Memoirs of Singlehood

And The Steps Toward Marriage

A Personal Journey of Regaining Hope, Purity and How to Love Again

---

By: Ericka Glorious Moore

Dedication

10.25.12
10:10 p.m.

My older sister and I were watching an episode of my favorite show "Everybody Loves Raymond" and the episode was about marriage. The mother and father had been married for 46 years. Tonya made this statement during the show, "When you move into the house you have your way and he has his way, but at some point you both have to get to Yahweh."

I dedicate this book to my loving older sister, Tonya, who believed in me from the beginning of its conception and whom I know is still cheering me on from heaven with its completion. I love you and miss you more than you will ever know.

Love your sis,

Ericka

Table of Contents

Acknowledgements

I would like to first acknowledge and thank the Lord, Jesus Christ for healing my heart and giving me a fresh start in life. Without His mercy, forgiveness, grace and love this book would not have been possible.

I would like to acknowledge a very special woman, my mentor, Pastor Nancy Shannon. You were the first person I told about my desire to write this book. Thank you for your wisdom and advice through the years. You helped me become the woman I am today and gave me the courage to pen my life to paper. You have always believed the best about me even when at times I did not.

Thank you to my sisters Tonya, Tina (Parham) and Charmaine Moore, for encouraging me to complete this book, regardless of my past, so I can help others heal and succeed. Thank you to my illustrator, my twin sister, Michelle Gonzalez. You are a very talented artist and now the whole world will see it. A very special thank you to my friend and editor, Dr. Rakisha Sloane, for the many hours of meeting in person, on the phone, through text messages, several edits, continuous encouragement, and prayers to complete this project. Thank you for keeping me focused and organizing my thoughts. I know without you, I could not have accomplished any of this and I am forever grateful.

Thank you to a woman that has touched me from a distance, since the age of seventeen when I first saw you at my church, P. Bunny Wilson. Your books have inspired me to be a better woman, especially your book, Knight in Shining Armor. It encouraged me to step out and write about a difficult subject matter and to be transparent and vulnerable in my life.

I would also like to thank my friends who prayed and supported me on this journey, Jikhara Price, Shelle Burke, Amanda Fico and Stephanie Goode. Thank you to my church family at Family Harvest Church, Pastor Patty Plante and Dr. Robb and Linda Thompson.

And lastly, thank you to my wonderful parents. You have always been my cheerleaders since I was little and always will be. Love you dearly and I am extremely grateful to have you in my life.

Preface

In 2008, it was on my heart to write this book. Nine years later, you are reading the finished product. Below is my original journal entry:

5.15.2008

It has been about 3 years now since I gave away my most precious gift to a man I loved deeply. It wasn't my heart, mind, or soul, but it was my body...my virginity. We hear many people in the world nonchalantly give away this gift, but it is an awesome and valuable gift. It inhabits a woman from birth. It is a token of love that is given at the union of marriage before God. I decided to write this book not because I wanted to share my past, but so I can help women be free in their future. I heard Joyce Meyer say these words many years ago, "I go through the pain for someone else's victory."

Well here I am in the raw, to be transparent with you about my mistakes, the pain they caused, and how I fought my way out to victory. Many of you ladies reading this book may have lost your virginity because you believed a man loved you, or through rape, or molestation, but I am here to say you are a winner and you can make it through. As I pondered writing this book, I thought about all the stages I went through after losing my virginity. All you women that are still virgins, I commend you...stay strong. All you women that the gift was taken from you, I am here to tell you that there is hope, healing, and victory awaiting you. As you read these pages I pray you will be strengthened to trust God, believe who He said you are, and love yourself again. I'm not saying it is going to be easy but you can make it through stronger and one day you will share your testimony to help someone else.

Love,

Ericka Glorious Moore

Introduction

"All the single ladies, all the single ladies!" If you are holding this book, I would assume you are a single woman who has an interest in being married. Or you may be a married woman looking for ways to help the single women in your life. Whatever your state, I believe you will enjoy the scenery of my past landscapes of silly stories of pursuing, getting engaged, healing to mend my broken heart, all leading up to the road I am currently traveling to be prepared for my king at the end of the road, my Knight in Shining Armor.

This book will show you how I regained my focus to maximize my singlehood. It will address how to make better decisions, how to overcome past hurts, and what it means to be in a season of "preparation" with God. So sit back in your comfy chair, grab your favorite cup of joe, a journal, and join me on this fun journey of my life "Memoirs of Singlehood and the Steps Toward Marriage."

At the end of each chapter of our journey together, I will challenge you to start the journey to freedom. You will see questions that I want you to answer honestly and sincerely before you move to the next chapter. At some point you may want to share with someone you trust who can pray with you for complete healing.

Chapter 1

To Watch TV or Not (Watch) TV, That is The Question

Seat belt strapped and ready to go? Come with me on a little trip down memory lane. This is where it all began, watching a lot of television. One of my favorite movies as a young teen was "Sixteen Candles." Jake Ryan was the cute guy that noticed the (so she thought) unnoticeable Samantha. She dreamed about how nice it would be if he were her boyfriend. She even told her friend she would lose her virginity to him. He was the handsome rich guy any girl would fall for. It was the trademark ending that caught my attention, the scene when he came looking for her. He first went to her house, then to the church where her sister was getting married. All the cars slowly moved away and there stood Jake Ryan in front of his red Ferrari looking straight at Samantha. She turns around to see who he is looking for and is in complete shock when he mouths to her, "You." At the end he wishes her happy birthday and says, "Make a wish" to blow out the candles and she says, "My wish already came true," and he leans over and kisses her. Wow, what a great sixteenth birthday present! Naturally, after watching this movie, I thought this was supposed to happen when you turned sixteen. So guess what happened to me? It was my sixteenth birthday and I planned to kiss the guy I was dating. We were at school by the lockers and there were people around watching us. Not at all like the movie! He kissed me and it was not bells and whistles, in fact it wasn't romantic at all, nor was it special. It was actually uncomfortable and a little embarrassing. But I imitated what I saw on the movie and I did not enjoy it.

WHAT YOU SEE IS WHAT YOU GET

I learned so many unhealthy things watching television that I had to choose to unlearn years later. We pick up the strangest beliefs and imitate what we see and hear from the craziest places. We get our beliefs from family, friends, and even teachers. We imitate what we see on TV, and/or radio and we begin to think these thoughts are true. These thoughts begin to shape who we are and determine the direction of our lives. Things going on around me and what I watched on the television played a huge part because I watched so much of it when I was young. There is a biblical proverb that says, "So a man thinks in his heart, so is he" (Proverbs 23:7). What you think about is what you will

66 What you think about is what you will ultimately become. 99

ultimately become. Besides thinking I was supposed to kiss on my sixteenth birthday, I picked up some negative thoughts that began to change the course of my life. I believed these thoughts for many years until I changed the way I thought about them.

I was talking to a friend and I mentioned to her that I had the opportunity to meet a 2-time Olympic medalist, Christine Magnuson, when she visited my local library. She talked about all the hours of training with her coach and how he trained her physically, but she also mentioned another coach she had in her journey to victory. She had a mental coach. The mental coach told her when she thought negative thoughts her muscles actually would get dense and would weigh more in the water and cause her to sink. She encouraged her to see herself winning and that her muscles would be lighter giving her a better chance to win. So you see, what you think, not only affects you mentally, but physically as well. Choose wisely what you watch with your eyes and what you listen to with your ears because you just might get it all, good or bad. So if you have a mind full of bad thoughts, don't be discouraged, be encouraged, because it can all change! Dr. Caroline Leaf, a neuroscientist and author of the 21-Day Brain Detox Challenge states, "The same way a thought is wired in, is the same way it can be wired out[1]."

Let's put into practice what I just discussed. Write down 1 or 2 negative thoughts that have bombarded your

&& What you think, not only affects you mentally, but physically as well. ??

mind for years and replace it with a positive thought. For example, if you have a thought that says, "You are a loser," you would replace it with "I am winner," or if the thought says, "You are ugly," you would say, "I am beautiful." This simple, yet profound principle is found in Philippians 4:8-9,

Summing it all up, friends, I'd say you'll do best by filling your minds and meditating on things true, noble, reputable, authentic, compelling, gracious—the best, not the worst; the beautiful, not the ugly; things to praise, not things to curse. Put into practice what you learned from me, what you heard and saw and realized. Do that, and God, who makes everything work together, will work you into his most excellent harmonies (MSG).

So get all the clutter out of your mind and begin to dream again and believe again for good things to come into your life. Wouldn't you rather have the good follow you rather than the negative? Understand this: The thought patterns of life can cause you to break down and compromise your standards, dreams and goals. If left unchallenged, these thoughts will follow you for the rest of your life, until you make a decision to change the way you think.

❝The thought patterns of life can cause you to break down and compromise your standards, dreams and goals. ❞

Freedom Challenge

- Have you ever been weighed down by thoughts of anger, defeat, unforgiveness, etc.?
- Did you see your life unfold and turn in a direction that you did not desire after holding on to wrong thought patterns?
- Write down a time in your life when you accomplished a dream or goal. What were some of the thoughts you were thinking to accomplish the dream or goal? How did you feel?

Before getting into the freedom prayer below, I wanted to give you the opportunity of true freedom to ask someone into your life to help you on your journey. He has been with me on my journey. His name is Jesus Christ. It was because of Jesus dying for my sins and giving His life for me that I have become the person I am today. You can know Him now, just like me. Romans 10:9-10 says to confess with your mouth that Jesus is Lord and believe in your heart that God raised Him from the dead and you will be saved.

So say this prayer out loud: Dear God in heaven, I come to you in the name of Jesus. I acknowledge to you that I am a sinner, and I am sorry for my sins and the life that I have lived; I need your forgiveness. I believe that your only begotten Son Jesus Christ shed His precious blood on the cross at Calvary and died for my sins, and I am now willing to turn from my sin. Father, I confess Jesus as the Lord of my life. With my heart, I believe that God raised Jesus from the dead. This very moment I accept Jesus Christ as my own personal Savior and according to His Word right now I am saved.

Freedom Prayer

Lord, I come before you today asking for your grace and mercy to help me change how I think about this negative thought _____and I replace it with this thought _____I know that you love me and want me free. I thank you in advance for the journey we are about to embark on through this book and you are right here with me through it all. Thank you in advance Holy Spirit for your comfort, wisdom and direction through this process and that I will reach my destination of freedom at the other end. Amen.

Chapter 2

Is That All I Am Is My Looks?

I was born a twin. I am the oldest by a whopping two minutes. And I make sure my sister knows it, even to this day! When my mother was pregnant with us, somehow in my mother's womb, my sister ended up on top of my head. When I was born I had a deformed shaped head. It was very pointy at the top. It was so misshaped the doctor wanted to do a surgical procedure where he would crack my skull to reshape my head to a normal shape. My mom was concerned about doing such a procedure and wanted to know the risks involved. The doctor explained that it could result in me being in a vegetative state. Because the back part of my skull was pliable and the front of my skull was already fused together, it would have been a risky surgery because technology and wearing helmets was not common at that time. My parents decided I would not have such a risky surgery. Needless to say, my head became a repeated center of attention for classmates to make fun of and this led to me having low self-esteem.

When it was time to go to school, I would have a sickening feeling in my stomach. I did not want to go to school at all. I loved my teachers but it was the students I dreaded being around. I loved to wear my hair in ponytails. I had very beautiful long black hair that went all the way down to my waist. I would style my hair in many ways with barrettes and ponytail holders. I was made fun of and bullied on a daily basis about the shape of my head and how I looked. I was so depressed I did not look in the mirror. My mom would allow me to stay home some days because I did not want to be made fun of. I didn't tell my teachers about what was happening.

> 66 *160,000 children miss school every year due to fear of attack or intimidation by other students.* 99

I'm not the only one that has felt this way. It is estimated that 160,000 children miss school every day due to fear of attack or intimidation by other students. The numbers are even higher for girls that deal with being harassed, 83 percent of girls and 79 percent of boys report experiencing harassment[2].

I remember I was in fourth grade and I had had enough. I decided I would just kill myself. I think I had heard somewhere at the time that one of the quickest ways to kill yourself was to slit your wrists. I figured it would be easier to just get this over with. I told my twin sister my plan. I went in the kitchen and grabbed a good ole' butter knife (that would not be able to cut me even if I wanted it to). I headed into the bathroom across from the kitchen and shut the door. Seconds after I entered the bathroom I heard my sister's voice say "Don't do it Ericka, don't kill yourself." I held the knife in my hand trying to figure out how I would do it. I thought long and hard about it. I even tried to slit my right wrist, but I realized I would need to use great force to break the skin. Eventually I opened the door, to my sister's delight I had not hurt myself. But I was still hurting so deep inside.

Many kids today deal with suicide after being repeatedly harassed and bullied at school. It is a major issue. According to Centers for Disease Control and Prevention (CDC) suicide was the third leading cause of death for young people ages 12–18 in 2007. In a typical 12-month period, nearly 14 percent of American high school students seriously consider suicide; nearly 11 percent make plans about how they would end their lives; and 6.3 percent actually attempt suicide. Another study on bullying states nearly 30 percent of students are either bullies or victims of bullying. According to this study, 10 to 14 year old girls may be at even higher risk for suicide[3].

"Nearly 30 percent of students are either bullies or victims of bullying."

Feeling like a freak at school had become the norm inside my mind. Not only did I not fit in because of how I looked with my misshaped head, I also did not fit in because of my ethnicity. At the time, I grew up in a neighborhood where the schools were attended by mostly white and black. There were not as many races and cultures as there are now in schools. I would either deal with jealousy because I had long pretty hair or I would be rejected because I did not look like I was white or black. I remember a time when I tried so desperately to be friends with a group of white girls at my school. They let me hang around them from time to time. One day, I was walking down the hallway with them when one of the girls said to me, "You know, we don't want you to hang around us anymore." They looked at me and walked away. I was absolutely crushed and heartbroken after that. I felt alone as I stood in the empty hallway. Alone is how I felt for most of my elementary school years. I was also unsure of myself, I felt isolated and rejected. I also felt I was the object of ridicule and a laughing stock. Seven out of ten girls believe they are not good enough or don't measure up in some way, including their looks, school performance and relationships with friends and family members[4].

Upward and onward! I graduated and made it to high school with a big low self-esteem sign on my head. It was right in the beginning of the school year and I walked upstairs onto the second floor only to run into a guy standing there. He was tall and had a light complexion. I will never forget what he said to me. He looked at me and said, "You're beautiful." I remember looking behind me and all around and I pointed to myself and said, "Are you talking to me?" He said, "Yes, I think you are beautiful." I could not recall a boy telling me that before in my life. I remember being so excited to get home that day. As soon as the school bus dropped me off I ran home as fast as I could. I ran upstairs into the kitchen and said, "Mom guess what? A guy said I was BEAUTIFUL!" My mom smiled and calmly responded, "Of course, you are beautiful." Unbeknownst to me, I was beautiful the whole time. I would slowly begin to realize this more during my high school years.

Tim will never realize how much those words would mean to me. I can recall that day as if it were yesterday.

This was the beginning of how I thought I truly looked would emerge. I still had people making fun of me, and bullying me every day. I would go to my history class and would sit across from this guy that would use his hands to make a deformed shape to represent my head every time he saw me. He shot down my beautiful bubble that I began to experience with Tim by affirming the ugly Ericka that so many people in elementary school pointed out.

I came to high school with the understanding that it was all about how you looked. Driving on my journey now takes me to my first roadblock of life and inner belief. It does not matter if you have brains, talent, or wit. It all boils down to your looks. Up until this point in my life, that is all it seemed to be about. I was made fun of how I looked and then the tables began to turn, I began to be accepted by how I looked. I began to make sure I dressed the best; I made sure I said things perfectly, just to fit in with everybody, even at the expense of not being myself. I began to be an actor of my own life. Playing two parts, myself on the inside but someone else outside. My belief was, it did not matter if I was happy, just conform and be what everybody else wants you to be and that's how you will fit in and be accepted.

❝Roadblock and inner belief. It does not matter if you have brains, talent or wit. It all boils down to your looks. ❞

Freedom Challenge

- Is there a time that you can relate to not being accepted by how you looked?
- Did you feel like you could not fit in?
- Do you know that you are beautiful just the way you are?
- Write down 3 or 4 things that you love about yourself in 5 minutes or less.
- Now, I want you to look at yourself in the mirror and say, "I love you."

Freedom Prayer

Lord, you have created me wonderfully and perfectly down to the detail of my hair color, skin, ethnicity, and race. You gave me my laugh, personality, and talents and I will not allow myself or anyone else to make me feel ashamed about who I am and who you created me to be. I thank you for the courage to stand up and simply be me in Jesus' name. Amen!

Chapter 3

Am I Ugly Or What?

fter college it seemed there was a decline in the interest of my beauty and what people thought about me. Not that I did not think I was pretty, but it seemed that guys were not approaching me anymore. Because I formed a belief system that was all about my looks I really felt like I lost my identity. So when that belief system was threatened, my insecurities grew more.

It was through my looks where I formed my validation and love from people. Joyce Meyer calls this "approval addiction", where you need to be affirmed on a daily basis with compliments, encouragement, and validation in order to know your worth. If no one commented on anything about me I would feel worthless. If I wore a new outfit or a pair of shoes and no one commented on them, I sometimes would not wear those items again. I based my life on people and it was an emotional roller coaster ride of ups and downs.

There was a time when I was at church and I had my hair in a high curly ponytail. I wore this particular hairstyle all the time. I also thought I was very pretty when

I did. I overheard a girl talking to her friend about me. She said my hair looked like a bird's nest. After hearing those words, I felt so ugly. In fact, I did not wear that hairstyle for a while after that comment and I also did not think I was pretty when I would. Another incident occurred when I went to the mall. I was on one end of the mall and a guy from the opposite direction screamed "Hey girl with the big ole' booty!" I was absolutely humiliated when I heard this. I remember going home and deciding I was going to starve myself. I did not eat for days and my mom told me she did not want an anorexic in her house. She said she was going to make me eat.

At that point, I hated who I was. I asked God, "Why would you make me this way?" I was being made fun of either way. No matter if I looked pretty or ugly, people would not leave me alone. It was during these times I would use my ways of escapism. These roadblocks that I knew so well would become my normal. I felt those were things I could control. As the pain of rejection, loneliness, fear, and stress grew so did my addictions. I was addicted to television and people's approval. I would run to those roadblocks that further hindered my progress in life. But I have good news. Hope was around the bend. We'll touch on that a little later.

> **As the pain of rejection, loneliness, fear and stress grew, so did my addictions.**

Freedom Challenge

- Have you created ways to cope with rejection, fear, shame, guilt, etc.? For example, do you eat or don't eat to numb the pain away?
- Do you drink, take drugs, or have sex? If you said yes, write down your coping mechanisms and ask yourself what are you running away from?
- Then write what it is you are really looking for. Is it love, acceptance, or validation?
- Think about healthy ways you can obtain these things and the path you can take to get there.

Freedom Prayer

Father, there is nothing in my life that is too big for you. You know everything about me. I thank you for being the Lord over my life and I make you the Lord over everything. I give you every fear, hurt and pain that has hurt me up until this point in my life. I want true freedom. I don't want to pretend to be free; I want to be free in you. You said whom the Son sets free, is free indeed. Thank you Father. Amen.

Chapter 4
....

What's Wrong With The Dating and Romance Thing When I Am Young?

When you were young, to have a boyfriend and to be in love was what most girls dreamed about. We also thought about the Disney fairy tale wedding we would have one day, the beautiful house with the white picket fence, and the two and half kids. A lot of times, it's what we think and breathe on a consistent basis. I mentioned earlier that I thought I was supposed to kiss on my sixteenth birthday. I also thought it was normal to have a boyfriend, kiss, touch, hang out, and date.

Well, what's so wrong with it anyway you may ask? In high school and college emotions and hormones are raging like crazy. Guys are busting at the seams with testosterone looking to find their next lady to release their pent up hormones. And girls are looking for love, affection and attention. The problem with this is that boundaries get crossed, feelings get hurt, and standards get broken.

I was nineteen years old when a very handsome man walked into my church. I remember being mesmerized by how good-looking he was. After getting to know him through a friendship, I decided to go further and give it a chance with him. Our relationship was on and off for five years. He romanced me and swept me off my feet. Chocolates, teddy bears, handwritten notes, cards, and flowers, he did so many things for me. I had someone that was paying attention to me and for the first time, it seemed like it was about more than my looks and for once, I really felt loved.

VALIDATION IS INTERNAL NOT EXTERNAL

The problem with dating and romance is if you are not ready for marriage, there is no reason to enter into a relationship with a man. "He who finds a wife finds what is good and receives favor from the Lord" (Proverbs 18:22, NIV, emphasis added). With this particular relationship, he knew he wanted to marry me, but I wasn't ready to get married. I wanted to just date and get to know him. We did not start off on the same page. I was a young naive college student learning about life and he was an experienced older man who knew the direction he wanted to go in life. So then why did I stay? Well I really believed that I loved him. He validated me continuously and affirmed me. Something I wanted to have and longed for. I

> **"The problem with dating and romance is if you are not ready for marriage, there is no reason to enter into a relationship with a man."**

was afraid to let him go, because I didn't know if I would have someone as great as him in my life. The problem was I wasn't ready to date, let alone ready for marriage.

After I graduated college, I had a horrible thing happen. I realized I had $26,000 in credit card debt that a family member racked up while I was in school. They asked me to take a few cards out in my name promising they would pay the monthly bills. Only to my dismay the cards were overdrawn and bouncing left and right. I found this out at 23 and I had to file bankruptcy at the age of 26. Everything in my life seemed to fall apart. I was hurting and I had a boyfriend that continually said he loved me and that I was beautiful. I mentioned this part of my life, because it is why I gave away one of the most valuable gifts I ever had.

Freedom Challenge

- Have you ever done something for someone else not caring how it made you feel because you wanted to be accepted?
- Have you ever been scared to be yourself for fear of not being accepted?
- Do you have a fear of men or a man and do not know how to say no to them?
- Read in your Bible, 1 Corinthians 7:1 and Song of Solomon 8:4. What do these scriptures mean to you?

Freedom Prayer

    I am bold and courageous as a lion. I run to You Father God, who is the strength of my life. I am victorious, because that is who you are to me. I can overcome anything in your name! I choose to look at the things I can change and not the things I can't. I give you all hurt and pain in Jesus' mighty name. Amen!

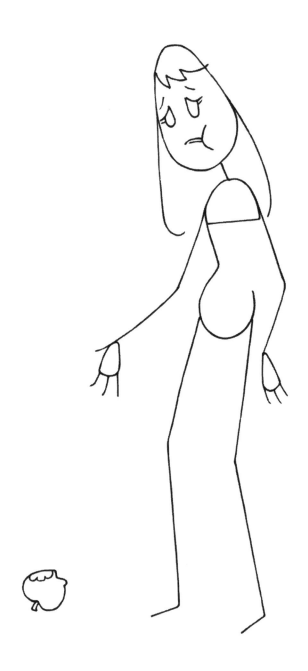

Chapter 5

Forbidden Fruit Isn't So Sweet

The DAY. Everything I believed about guys and my biggest fears were realized on this day. It was the day I lost trust in men. The day issues with authorities would escalate. The day I began to live in suspicion of people's motives. The day I lost myself. It was the day I lost my virginity. Although this happened many years ago, it was a painful journey to get to the place today to talk about it. I wish I could tell you that it was a magical experience. I also wish I could tell you it was the best thing that ever happened to me. But it wasn't, in fact I didn't want to lose my virginity at all. Do you know one-third of women regret how they lost their virginity? Hollywood glorifies that every girl is happy and that it so romantic, but usually when a girl chooses to lose her virginity before marriage it is because she is trying to fill the void of a deeper internal pain.

I had recently filed for bankruptcy and I was very vulnerable as a result. I longed so desperately for many years to feel safe with someone, anyone, and to feel loved. Being with my boyfriend at the time seemed like the safest place to be. I remember when it was all said and done; I couldn't believe what had happened. It was quick, but life changing. It was a horrible experience. I knew I did something terribly wrong. I immediately felt different, like part of me was missing.

Shame, guilt, anger, condemnation, brokenness, fear, and unworthiness were the feelings I dealt with all at the same time after it happened. I felt I would never be the same. I went into a state of depression for several months. I cried all the time. I became a shell of a person. Up until then, my belief system was built upon my looks and how to be perfect. The one thing I felt that gave me value was gone. This began my next set of roadblocks where I began to believe I was "damaged goods" and I would never amount to anything because of my poor decisions.

I was a Christian for many years before I lost my virginity. But I ran away from God. One thing I now understand after looking back is with God you can run, but you can't hide. He will never allow you to run away from your problems. He will actually do the opposite. He will have you confront them so you can be free.

For many years I was angry and unforgiving toward an authority figure in my life. I even stayed in the relationship with my boyfriend, even though I compromised all of my standards to stay there. I was miserable and I didn't know any way out. I ran deeper into my escape tactics. For the next several years I went through nine different cycles after the loss of my virginity. I would compare this

❝I began to believe that I was "damaged goods" and I would never amount to anything because of my poor decisions.❞

experience to people who go through cycles of grief of a loved one that has passed away.

The Bible says in Hebrews 11:25 that sin has pleasure for a season. So although you think you are having fun and enjoying the wrong, it is important to recognize there are consequences after losing your virginity. Here are some of the cycles you may have experienced and what I faced.

❝It is important to recognize that there are consequences after losing your virginity.❞

1. Unforgiveness - I believed God did not forgive me. I lived with this for years until I began to let God in to heal me. I was the last person to forgive myself because I believed I knew better, especially being a Christian.

2. Anger - When I lost my virginity I was so hard on myself. I would look at myself in the mirror and say, "I hate you." I would actually hit myself because I was so angry about my poor decision. I also hated my boyfriend because I believed he could have prevented it.

3. Shame and Embarrassment - I lived in horrible shame and embarrassment, I felt my life was a joke, and that I would never be good enough for anyone.

4. Soul Tie - God created sex for marriage because of the soul tie that is formed. Since I had sex with my boyfriend before marriage and then we broke up, I had to deal with the bond that was created. It took two years to break free from the heartache of that relationship.

5. Restitution (want to make things right) - I stayed in the relationship way too long. Women want reconciliation in every area of their life. That is why some women will stay in abusive relationships, or have multiple babies

with the same cheating man because he says he loves her and will be there for her. She is looking for restitution, but sometimes that will never come. She is also looking for her virginity to return, but it never will.

6. Depression - I went into a deep depression. I walked around empty and could be knocked down with a feather. My emotions were so fragile. I was so sad. I felt like I had nothing to give anyone.

7. Fear - Fear was extremely heightened and I did not trust anyone, especially men.

8. Inferiority - I was a coward with those around me. Because I viewed myself based off of my decisions and not what God said about me, I lacked confidence.

9. Pain of Rejection - The pain of rejection was so deep, I felt like I had nowhere to go, and that God didn't accept me and neither did men.

It took many years for me to forgive myself. It is the first out of the nine cycles, but it was the last one for me to get through. Maybe you have experienced one or all of these nine cycles and/or still are going through some of them. I want to encourage you, you will make it through to the other side! It is important to deal with this now in your life. It will never be a convenient time to go through pain and you don't want your future husband to pay for your unresolved baggage.

For you ladies who think losing your virginity is okay or a good idea, think again. The long-term effects from one moment of satisfaction can cause a lifetime of pain if not dealt with correctly. I was talking to a woman who lost her virginity at a young age. She had been picked on in school and had low self-esteem. She is married today with children, but still never dealt with the loss of her virginity. Clinical psychologist, Dr. Michael Mantell states becoming sexually active at an early age can have devastating lifelong consequences; it's a psychological disaster waiting to happen. It leads to empty relationships and low self-worth. The experience creates worry, regret, self-recrimination and guilt, loss of self-respect, shaken trust, depression, stunted personal development, damaged relationships, and relationship skills. It can also have a negative impact on marriage, should one ever take place. When a girl experiences sex early in life free of commitment, she learns an erroneous message that sex means nothing. Her experience is that nothing

happened as a result of her having sex, which creates the belief that sex and commitment have nothing to do with each other. Later this can be carried into marriage, where the girl may believe that sex is not an important part of marriage when, clearly, it is[5].

"When a girl experiences sex early in life free of commitment, she learns an erroneous message that sex means nothing."

Just because you get married does not mean you have dealt with the problem. It will arise later in life, especially when you have your own children. There are many reasons why you should wait until you get married. The obvious reasons are the risks of contracting HIV/AIDS, STDs, or getting pregnant, but the ultimate reason is, God created sex to be done in a committed and intimate relationship of marriage.

When a woman has sex outside of marriage she has given all of herself when she gives her body. When there is no commitment attached she feels naked, exposed physically and spiritually to the man she had sex with. This is called a soul tie. A man often loses respect for the woman he so often said he loved. Why? Because men don't want you to give up that gift either.

They want you to make them be in a committed relationship with them as well. Although this was a poor decision in my life and there were many consequences as a result, it has helped me to grow into who I am today. To encourage you, I believe you will overcome and be strong again in this area and with God's help you can have lasting relationships, feel secure and know you are loved by God and your loved ones.

Freedom Challenge

- Have you ever had a monumental day when a decision you made changed the direction of your life? Good or bad?
- Have you ever looked for a place, person or thing to feel safe?
- Write down a time when you felt that you could be yourself. Who were you with and where were you?
- If you have never experienced peace and safety, ask God for His perfect peace to touch your heart.

Freedom Prayer

Father, you said if I confess my sins to you, that you would forgive me and make me white as snow. I ask you to forgive me for doing this sin_____ and I repent and choose to never do it again. Thank you for your strength and helping me to stay on the right path, so I can bring you glory in everything I do. In Jesus' name. Amen!

Chapter 6

I Want To Be Married And
I Want It Now

I love going on mission trips. I have been going on trips since 2005. God has done mighty things in my life and the lives of others on every single trip, but one thing stood out to me most recently. I was talking to one of my girlfriends on the phone about my upcoming missions' trip to Puerto Rico. And then I had an "aha moment." On every trip, there was either a guy who ended up liking me or I ended up liking him. I never realized the distraction the devil put in my face until that moment. I believe it was because of my deep desire to get married and that is what I drew to me.

Although it was nice for a nano-second when a guy gave me attention, it wasn't fulfilling and those were not my motives for any of the trips. So this particular trip I decided I would not allow myself to be distracted by a guy. So, of course as soon as I made this declaration I had guys coming out the woodworks. It is interesting when you finally don't care about marriage it seems to come to the surface.

For many years I have longed to be married. I cried about it, whined to my friends about it, told my family about it, but to no avail, still no husband. I thought if I made my requests a thousand times to God maybe He would be moved, but...no. I had so many frustrations. I threw hissy fits. Then one day in all of my frustrations I took matters into my own hands. I rolled up my sleeves and went to the computer, tapped away at the computer and signed up for dating sites.

This brought more discouragement, because I did not see one guy I was interested in. I also decided to "be open." So I gave guys a try that I normally would not have thought about dating. Through each relationship, even though they didn't work out I did learn a lot more about myself that I needed to work on. There were also qualities from them that I liked. I heard many people say to me, "just be open, God knows what you want, but He also knows what you need." People would even tell me he could be ugly, because I could be an answered prayer for him to have a beautiful wife. Some advice was helpful, but some was not.

> **"Would I ever get married? Are my standards too high? Does the guy I want really exist?"**

At times this caused depression, anxiety and doubt to creep in and these questions rang loud and clear in my ears. Would I ever get married? Are my standards too high? Does the guy I want really exist? I pondered these questions several times throughout the day. I think at one point I was obsessed with marriage. But with all the crying, fearing, kicking and screaming, and begging for a husband one word came to mind, "motive." Why did I want to get married so badly? Here are some of my reasons:

- I wanted to be loved and to love someone.
- I wanted validation.
- I wanted companionship.
- I wanted someone to hold me and tell me everything would be okay.
- I wanted someone to show me affection and to be affectionate with.

When I took the time to evaluate all my motives, I realized they were pretty selfish reasons to get married. Not one thing on the list showed I wanted to help my husband with his dreams and goals, serve him the rest of my life and ensure I would make his life easier. Marriage is all about sacrifice and laying down one's life. Marriage is actually one of the most selfless commitments for two people. It's also important to remember your future husband is not there to fix everything wrong that happened to you, or to repair your hurting heart from all the wrong guys before you meet him. He is not coming to make you happy. A man doesn't want a girl that is broken and doesn't know her value. He wants her whole, complete and confident. And the only way you get this way is through God and His righteousness. Only God can heal you, make you whole without anything missing or broken. And He is your complete joy.

So for the first time in my life, I was not looking to be married. Yes, the desire was still there, but it was not the priority. I

❝A man doesn't want a girl that is broken and doesn't know her value. He wants her whole, complete and confident.❞

casted the care on God and I patiently rested in His arms, finally able to enjoy being single. A scripture came to mind during this time where it says, "Let your conversation be without covetousness; and be content with such things as ye have: for he hath said, I will never leave thee, nor forsake thee" (Hebrews 13:5, KJV, emphasis added).

I have made a decision to be content with God. For many years I would covet what others had and what I didn't have. This caused me to be ungrateful for all the wonderful things God did do in my life. Although I wished God would move on my speed and do it my way, I knew if I would have had my way, I may be divorced, broke and miserable right now. I was not ready and God knows the plans He has for me to give me a hope and a future and not to harm me. So I thank God every day for "The Day." I thank God I woke up "Today" and I have family and friends today. I have a job, a great church, I can pay my bills, and I am healthy "today." And for the first time I actually love myself and my life.

Ladies, how many of you have felt the exact same way or can relate to something I just said? I know it may seem difficult now, but it will all be worth it when you decide to wait on God and His perfect will for your life. Do not settle and give up on your dream to be married. According to Psalm 37:4, God put the desire in your heart in the first place and it is up to Him to make it come to pass. Just keep your eyes focused on Him in heaven and sure enough you will run smack dab into your future husband here on the earth. Be encouraged!

Freedom Challenge

- List 1 or 2 things that stood out to you.
- Do you think about marriage every day or often?
- Do you feel discouraged or doubtful that marriage will ever happen for you?
- Write down something that excites you for the day you get married?
- Write down a scripture that you can use to encourage yourself to keep believing and hoping in God no matter where you are in life.

Freedom Prayer

God, I believe your plan is perfect and I believe in your perfect timing. There is no lack of guys, because there is no lack with you. I will wait patiently for my prince; because I know when he comes it will be worth the wait. I thank you in advance for the wonderful testimony of your faithfulness and goodness in my life. In Jesus' name. Amen.

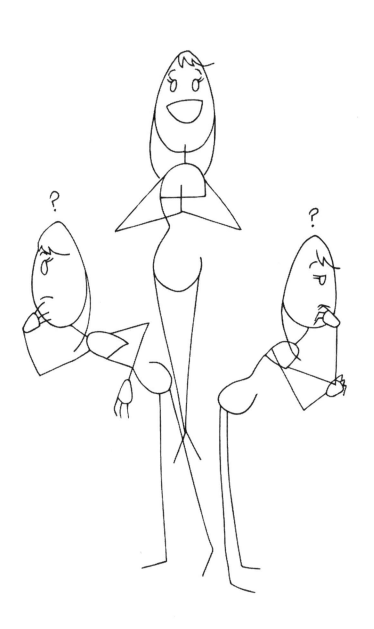

Chapter 7

....

This Way, That Way...Ultimately Only God's Way

I was around 20 years old when I met a guy who was a fantastic pianist and a friend of a mutual friend. I was not attracted to him at all, but he liked me a lot. All of sudden I started having dreams about him and in the dreams I kept hearing I was going to marry him, but I wasn't happy about it. In fact, it actually scared me. All during the day and night I couldn't run away from the haunting thoughts of this man. In the previous chapter I mentioned people would tell me maybe I would marry someone who was ugly. Well this guy was not the most attractive person in the world and I became afraid I would actually marry him. So I began running away from the thought in my mind and I ran right into the arms of my ex-fiancé. I figured here at least I was safe.

During the beginning of my relationship with my ex-fiancé I was on cloud nine. We had a lot of wonderful times together. He was older than me and would tell me so many interesting stories and share his experiences with me. We both had big dreams we thought would collide together one day and form a fantastic marriage. But there were a few things that happened right at the beginning of our relationship that caused it to spiral out of control by the end. Experience Principle: The breakdown in any relationship is the breakdown of character and boundaries.

My ex-fiancé knew I wanted my first kiss at the altar. He also knew I was a virgin and how important it was to share that with my husband. On our first date we kissed. First boundary I allowed to be crossed. I became afraid to speak up for myself when my boundaries would get crossed. I had learned to sacrifice my feelings for the sake of someone else's since elementary school. One day he put his hand on my knee. I was extremely uncomfortable about it, but I didn't say anything. He would put his hand around my waist, I didn't like it, but I allowed it. Inside I was a nervous wreck about how uncomfortable I was, but I was so afraid to speak up because I didn't want him to get mad. I learned how to wear a mask on my face and make sure everybody believed I was happy. So I learned to hide behind the mask and keep up a masquerade that everything was okay.

Fast forward several years later and the relationship was over and I had to deal with all the baggage that came along with it. One thing was consistent in all my relationships with guys up to this point was I allowed them to cross my boundaries, even if it made me feel uncomfortable. I felt I was less than them. Whenever a guy seemed disappointed or upset with me, I would start to panic, get anxious and be afraid. I automatically thought I was in trouble.

I had to make some life altering decisions at this point in my life, by asking myself these questions. Would I allow myself to continue to repeat the same mistakes in relationships? Would I have the courage to confront the pain and hurt inside so God could truly set me free from bondage in relationships that I put myself in? Would I continuously choose a guy based on my own needs of being fulfilled, such as validation, acceptance and love? Or would I choose God's plan and trust He has my life in His hands? Would I choose God's way or my way?

" Would I choose God's way or my way? "

THE ALTIMA (ULTIMATE) LIST

On my way to work one day, I got into a car accident and my car was totaled. It was in the middle of winter, so it was an inconvenient time to look for a new one. But I was excited because I could get my dream car, a Nissan Altima. I wanted this car for six years. I wanted a Bose radio, heated leather seats, remote start, and I wanted a convertible top in pearl white. I pulled into the Nissan dealership so excited to drive the car I wanted for so long. Something odd happened though, when the salesman pulled up the car, my first reaction was disappointment. Inside me, I didn't understand why I felt so down about the car of my dreams. We went for a test drive. Still disappointed. The salesmen, who reminded me of Nicholas Cage, said I thought you always wanted this car. I said I thought so too but I am not excited anymore. We also test drove the Nissan Maxima. He even let me keep the Altima for a day. He thought my mind would change. I sought God about what was going on inside. What happened was my desires had changed over the last six years. I realized I was not the same and neither was what I wanted. So I told God, I don't know what car I want, so show me what I want. I ended up with a Chevy Cruze, with all the bells and whistles of the Altima, but this was a brand I had never considered before my heart changed. So guess what happened next?

❝Open to all the possibilities. Open to God's best for me, whatever package that comes in. ❞

I thought about my ideal hus-band. For years I wanted my husband to be of a specific ethnicity, everyone around me knows I have desired this. I also, had a list I wrote years ago with all the things I wanted in my future mate. After the car ordeal, I told God, I want what you want me to have. I recognized I was a different woman from several years ago and I wouldn't want him to come and then I am disappointed. So now I am open. Open to all the possibilities. Open to God's best for me, whatever package that comes in.

Freedom Challenge

- Ladies, have your ever felt like you were in a cycle that was producing negative results, but you did not know how to get out of it?
- Have you been in a relationship with a man knowing it was not what you really wanted?

- Have you compromised your standards to be in a relationship? How did it make you feel?
- Are you ready to trust God with every area of your life knowing He only wants the best for you?
- Do you trust God's perfect will for your life?

Freedom Prayer

Lord, I know at times I have not believed your plan for my life. I also know I have wanted my way. But I tell you now I only want your way. Because your way is the best way. It is the perfect way. I choose to trust you for the husband you have for me and I know he will be better than I can possibly think or imagine. I give you all the praise for changing me and making me who you want me to be. In your precious, Holy name. Amen.

Chapter 8

Prep School 101: Time to Get Your House In Order

Broken, lonely, and hurt. I remember how I felt after the relationship ended with my ex-fiancé. I thought to myself, "I will never allow myself to go through that kind of pain again." I made a decision that I wanted God involved in every area of my life. One of the first things I had to do was repent to the Lord for doing things my way and not trusting His Word. Repentance means to turn from thinking your own way and agreeing with God's Word about a matter. The Bible clearly states, "If we confess our sins, He is faithful and just to forgive us our sins, and to cleanse us from all unrighteousness" (1 John 1:9, KJV, emphasis added). I told God, please would you just knock me over the head when my husband comes and say "This is him," because I didn't want to hurt anyone else, or be hurt.

After several years of being single, I went to my mentor and pastor and she told me I was in a season of preparation for marriage. This was in 2008. She said for me to ask God what to do and how to prepare. All you single ladies, when someone says you are in a season of preparation, what would you think? Well I thought marriage was right around the corner for me. Fast-forward nine years later and I am still sitting here waiting. I guess the season needed to last a lot longer than I expected!

It has been an interesting journey during the last nine years, but I wouldn't trade it for the world. God has had me read books on marriage and single women preparing for marriage. I journal a lot, so I was able to get out a lot of pain and built up hurt. I acknowledged offense in my heart and asked God to forgive me and help me to forgive those that hurt me. I interviewed several married women and asked their advice about marriage, which you will read in the next chapter. I learned to speak up for myself if someone crossed my boundaries, and I created standards again that I wouldn't allow people to cross.

BRING IT INTO THE LIGHT

I remember when God put it on my heart to tell someone I lost my virginity. It was a few years ago, but I felt like I really needed to tell them. So I did, and even though I cried my eyes out, freedom came. Then the first guy I dated after my relationship, God told me to tell him, and I did, and more freedom came.

One day, the Lord put it on my heart to tell my two sisters. My older sister already knew, but I felt ashamed about telling my other sisters. They seemed so proud that I was a virgin and I felt I was on a pedestal that would come crashing down if I told them I really wasn't a virgin. I didn't want to disappoint them, but I wanted to come clean and not let them believe a lie. We were at my parents' house in their bedroom and I told them. Their responses were so kind. They didn't judge me or make me feel bad, but they embraced me and loved me. And with that it brought me complete freedom. Now, those that are reading this book know and it is okay with me. I recognize if I knew back then, what I know now, yes of course my life would be completely different, but I didn't and that's okay.

If you have had trouble telling people about your past mistakes because you are scared of what they will think, who cares! Be transparent, God loves it when we are. He says, "But you desire honesty from the womb, teaching me wisdom even there" (Psalm 51:6). I've learned that God knows what is in our hearts anyway, so we might as well tell Him.

> **" *A man doesn't want a girl that is broken and doesn't know her value. He wants her whole, complete and confident.* "**

Of course, don't go shouting to the rooftops all the horrible things you've done. What I am saying is, if there is a sin keeping you bound sometimes the best way to get free is to just tell on yourself and be done with it once and for all.

GETTING IT ALL OUT IN THE OPEN

Since we are talking about bringing everything into the light, I wanted to pull over for a pit stop and talk about an area that is taboo and rarely discussed these days. Maybe you didn't lose your virginity, but you may have or currently deal with masturbation. More often than not, girls are walking around with this "dirty little secret" with overwhelming guilt and shame and dare not tell anyone they are dealing with this issue. In fact, the National Survey of Sexual Health and Behavior (NSSHB) conducted a study involving more than 800 teens, aged 14 to 17 years, nearly three-quarters of boys surveyed reported having ever masturbated and slightly less than half among girls[6].

You may ask, what is wrong with masturbation? Well, masturbation is having sex with yourself. And although it is done in a private setting it can have very open consequences if not addressed. It also can produce some of the following issues in your life and your future marriage such as, being selfish or addicted to other sexual behaviors, and your future spouse will have a hard time pleasing you in the bedroom.

Author P.B. Wilson asks the question in her book, Knight in Shining Armor, "Why is masturbation so destructive to a satisfying sex life once couples are married?" Because it is self-gratifying, and no one knows our bodies as well as we do. A person who masturbates knows exactly how his or her body is stimulated, the right amount of pressure to be applied, and the thoughts that bring an orgasm. When that person gets married there is no way another human being will know exactly what will satisfy him or her. And, if the person getting married assumes their partner should know or doesn't understand how God's sexual principles work, even greater unfulfillment and frustration will follow. Many times these husbands and wives resort to masturbating even though they are married[7].

One last area I want to bring into the light before moving on is pornography. Pornography can cause a lot of issues as well if not dealt with properly. It creates impossible expectations of sex, unattainable fantasies with another person, and selfishness to name a few. When we watch images that were never intended for us to see we only think about what we want, how we want others to act and what we want them to do for us. Just like masturbation, it is hard for another person to satisfy you, because you have become so accustomed to satisfying the needs yourself, they can never obtain the unreasonable expectations you have placed on them.

If you are trying to overcome the challenges of masturbation or pornography you can be free. You do not have to hold your head in a cloud of shame and guilt, nor do you have to learn how to cope with it. It is time to confess it out to God and if you feel the need to, confess it out to someone you trust. Over the years, I had other areas I dealt with and got free from by doing this. I remember how much guilt and shame I felt for having problems, especially being a Christian. But when God had me confess it to others (I trusted), guess what? The devil could not use it against me anymore, because it was in the light and out in the open. Scripture states, "Confess your sins to each other and pray for each other so that you may be healed. The earnest prayer of a righteous person has great power and produces wonderful results." (James 5:16, NLT, emphasis added). The Word says that healing comes when we confess our sins one to another and we have wonderful results when a righteous person is in prayer and agreement for our freedom and healing. You are not alone, so confide in someone you trust, confess your sins and be healed.

66 The earnest prayer of a righteous person has great power and produces wonderful results. 99

CONFRONT THE HURT

In chapter two, I talked about an authority figure who asked me to take out credit cards in my name which led to me being $26,000 in debt and forced me to file bankruptcy at the age of 26. During my preparation time for marriage, God had me go back to confront the pain. The authority had apologized over and over throughout the years after it happened, but I still had unresolved hurt. It caused so many problems.

The first thing I did was ask God to help me to forgive that authority figure. This scripture helped me to forgive, be kind to each other, tenderhearted, forgiving one another, just as God through Christ has forgiven you (Ephesians 4:32, NLT). Second, I chose to look at the situation through their eyes. By doing this I was more compassionate. Third, I went to a program called "Celebrate Recovery."

The day I finally forgave myself, the Lord spoke to me and said, "I forgave you the first day you asked me."

It was another outlet to get my feelings out around other women without feeling judged or condemned. They just allowed me to speak and they listened. Fourth, I took responsibility for my choices and actions. It took many years to heal, but I can honestly say all the hurt is gone with that authority figure. Along the way, I was also freed from other wrong ways of thinking and unhealthy habits.

FORGIVE

I had made some great strides in moving forward with my life, but one of the most important and hardest things I had to do was forgive myself. I hated myself. I beat myself up every day for years about my decisions. I thought I had messed up so bad that God could never love a person like me. But since I had chosen to do things God's way and not my own, I needed to believe what He said about me. He said He loves me no matter what according to first John 1:9 and He is faithful and just to forgive me when I confess my sins to Him. The day I finally forgave myself, the Lord spoke to me and said, "I forgave you the first day you asked me."

I mentioned in chapter five many of the consequences I faced, some of them I still face today. I know I am forgiven and God has forgiven me, but there are some lingering effects from the choices I made in my past. I know one day, whenever I do have children I will have to explain to them why mommy wasn't a virgin when she got married. I also can't give that gift to my future husband. But what I can give to my husband will be purity. I also know I am the righteousness of God and I am pure in His sight. Have you forgiven yourself over past situations and hurts? If not, today is your day to finally do so.

STANDARDS REESTABLISHED

Before I lost my virginity, I desired to have a man who was also a virgin. I also didn't want to kiss my husband until we were at the altar. Well I failed at doing both of those standards. But it didn't mean I couldn't keep moving forward toward accomplishing those standards. So, progress is being made. The Bible says in Proverbs 24:16, a righteous man falls down seven times, but he gets back up. I have been celibate since my ex-fiancé. I have also been in relationships where I have not kissed the guy on the lips, so I take my victories with each step of the way. I wrote down a list of standards and the kind of man I wanted and gave it to those I respect and will not allow me to compromise. I learned how to speak up for myself when I felt uncomfortable and when I am in compromising situations. I have learned to be honest with myself and with others. I have also learned to keep my boundaries and standards. I now know my value and God loves me and I have chosen to love myself. I can have whatever I want.

> **"I now know my value and that God loves me and I have chosen to love myself."**

ENJOYING LIFE, ENJOYING ME

Now on to some fun things I began to do during my preparation for marriage. I started to take baths once a week; I also took care of my feet and nails. I wanted to be in the habit of having soft skin and smelling good for my husband. I had date nights with God on Friday nights. It was so much fun. I would talk to God, read the Bible, confess the Word, and ask Him for His direction and guidance. I was excited for date nights. I wanted to know God in a greater way and I did.

One thing that was huge for me, and my friends could attest to, I started to enjoy my life and who God made me to be. I started to finally feel comfortable in my own skin. For years, I was bound and broken and lived in so much shame. But now I was free. I began to be open with guys and give them chances. I would invite people over and host parties. I learned to think more about what God thought and cared less about what people thought of me. I have fun in my life now, I laugh, I have hope for my future, and I look forward to my future with excitement. Ladies, it's time for you to start living your life and being what God called you to be.

> **❝I learned to think more about what God thought and cared less about what people thought of me.❞**

ℱreedom 𝒞hallenge

- Are you comfortable in your own skin? Are you free to be yourself without fear of rejection?
- Are you enjoying your life?
- Have you forgiven yourself and others that have hurt you?
- What is something that stood out to you in this chapter that you can apply to your own life?
- Write down one thing you will do each week that is fun for you and do it. A few examples are going to a movie with your friends, inviting friends over and hanging out, getting a pedicure, or going on a vacation. Whatever you decide, just have fun!

Freedom Prayer

Father, I am ready to enjoy my life with all the imperfections, because in you I am spotless and have no sin. I choose to love my life, and others and make the most out of every opportunity that comes my way. I believe I can do anything, because you are with me and make it possible. I am ready to step into all that you have called me to be in Jesus' name. Amen.

Chapter 9

Renew Your Mind...It Does a Body Good

In the previous chapter, I explained my process to be free. Let me emphasize how this freedom came. My freedom came because I reached a point when I finally believed what God said about me, instead of how I felt about myself. So, to do this, I had to learn to replace my thoughts with God's thoughts. I talked about this briefly in chapter one. This is what caused me to renew my mind. Romans 12:1-2 says, "Be ye therefore transformed by the renewing of your mind and be not conformed to this world, but conformed by the written Word of God that you may know his perfect will for your life." Some of the ways I learned to replace my thoughts with God's thoughts was through journaling, confessing, meditating, and reading the Word of God.

My mentor taught me this very important exercise. Get a journal and write all your thoughts good, bad, or ugly for five minutes, then go back and read what you wrote. If you see any thought contrary to the Word of God, then replace the thought with a scripture. So when thoughts would come to me and say "God can never love a person like me." I would write the scripture reference next to the thought that says, nothing can separate me from the love of God (Romans 8:38). This exercise helped me change the way I thought in many areas of my life. I could recognize quickly what was happening in my mind and combat it with the Word. There was a time when fear seemed so big in my life and it was overtaking me. By journaling,

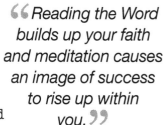

" *Reading the Word builds up your faith and meditation causes an image of success to rise up within you.* "

I saw that I wasn't fearful in every area of my life, but it could have been fear about a situation at work or a confrontation I needed to make in a relationship. So God would show me it was only two things that I needed to deal with, not that I was a fearful person.

Have you felt like you were angry, depressed or fearful? I bet, after trying this exercise out for a few days in a row, you will see that it may be only one or two things that are really bothering you. Doing this exercise may take away the feelings of being overwhelmed and give you courage to fight back.

Once I knew what scriptures to stand on for the day I would confess with my mouth the Word of God when those negative thoughts would come throughout the day. God's Word says in Romans 5:17, "Faith comes by hearing, and hearing by the Word of God." Eventually the thoughts would stop. I did this every day, sometimes several times in a day, until I got my mind to line up with the Word.

Reading the Word and meditating on the promises of

God is extremely important. Reading the Word builds up your faith and meditation causes an image of success to rise up within you. Joshua 1:8 says, "This Book of the Law shall not depart from your mouth, but you shall meditate in it day and night, that you may observe to do according to all that is written in it. For then you will make your way prosperous, and then you will have good success.

You can only go as far as your inner image. Proverbs 23:7 says, "So as a man thinks in his heart, so is he." If you think you will never amount to anything, you won't. Even with all the promises of God, you will still fail. It is important to keep your eyes on God at all times, no matter what comes your way. Renewing your mind is a daily process. Dr. Robb Thompson has said, "Your mind stays renewed as long as your hair stays combed." So that means it changes daily. You will be as successful, free, full of love, and excited about life, as you want to be. I saw myself as a failure for so many years, but God looked at me blameless and holy. You can have as much of God as you want to have. Are you ready to walk out your freedom?

The following scriptures helped me to walk in my freedom and healing. There is no sin that is too big for Him to forgive. You have been made right in His sight, after you confess your sins to Him. He accepts you and delivers you. He loves you right now in all your mistakes and mess. Even after all of my mistakes, He still loves me and has a plan for my life. So I encourage you to meditate on the scriptures below and begin to truly believe them about yourself, because God already believes them about you.

He Forgives You
Psalm 103:12 (ISV) says, "As distant as the east is from the west, that is how far he has removed our sins from us."

He Created You Brand New
2 Corinthians 5:17 (NKJV), Therefore, if anyone is in Christ, he is a new creation; old things have passed away; behold, all things have become new.

He Accepts You
Ephesians 1:6 (KJV), "To the praise of the glory of his grace, wherein he hath made us accepted in the beloved."

He Sees You Free of Sin
Colossians 1:22 (KJV), "In the body of his flesh through death, to present you holy and unblameable and unreproveable in his sight."

He's The God of Fresh Starts
Proverbs 24:16 (NIV), "For though the righteous fall seven times, they rise again, but the wicked stumble when calamity strikes.

He Has a Plan for Your Life
Jeremiah 29:11 (NLT), "For I know the plans I have for you," says the Lord. "They are plans for good and not for disaster, to give you a future and a hope."

He's Your Father
2 Corinthians 6:18 (NLT), "And I will be your Father, and you will be my sons and daughters, says the LORD Almighty."

He Loves You
Romans 8:38-39 (NLT), "And I am convinced that nothing can ever separate us from God's love. Neither death nor life, neither angels nor demons, [b] neither our fears for

today nor our worries about tomorrow—not even the powers of hell can separate us from God's love." 39, "No power in the sky above or in the earth below—indeed, nothing in all creation will ever be able to separate us from the love of God that is revealed in Christ Jesus our Lord."

Freedom Challenge

- Have you ever doubted that God loves you?
- Do you know that God loves you no matter what?
- Do you know that God has a plan for your life?
- Do you know you can overcome anything that has happened in your life?
- Do you know you that freedom awaits you and that you can walk in your purpose?

Freedom Prayer

Father, I know you love me because you sent your Son to die for me. I receive your love. I choose to believe that I am loved, whether I do things right and even when I fail. I look forward to having a deeper relationship with you and a greater revelation of your love for me. I am looking forward to a great future and with anticipation that I will make a difference in this world, because you made a difference in me. I love you and thank you for your faithfulness and for not giving up on me in Jesus' name. Amen.

Chapter 10

I Know You Have Something To Say

It has been nine years since Pastor Nancy told me I was in a season of preparation. Over these years, I have asked many questions from married women who I admire and esteem. What they had to say was extremely important and a great tool to help me when I get married. I asked five women who have been married anywhere between ten to fifty years, the following questions: "What are the greatest joys of marriage and if you had to do it over again what would you do?"

I wrote down their words and have pondered them throughout this preparation season. I thought it would be helpful for me to share some of their advice. Hopefully their wisdom will help and encourage you with your steps toward marriage. You will notice that some of the women have the same advice on some things, take note of that, I know I did.

Pearls of Wisdom from a woman married over fifty years. Who else can start you on the right track of getting ready for marriage, but your mom? What a great person to ask as a reference, because I saw my mom live it right in front of me. My mother's wisdom for marriage:

1. Remember to be flexible (make a schedule for your day, but if things change, because your husband has something different in mind, just go with the flow. Remember you are his helpmeet, not the other way around.

2. Don't sweat the small stuff. Meaning, if he likes to put sugar all over the counter after making his coffee, and you have told him a trillion times to clean it up, just clean it up and look at the things your husband does that are a blessing. It is not worth getting into strife and bitterness over sugar. Of course, you can apply this across every part of your life.

3. When you address your husband about an area and he promises that he will change it and then he doesn't, this does not mean that he does not respect you. Make sure to always trust God concerning your husband.

> *Learning the best time to talk to your husband will be something you must watch and learn about him.*

4. Learn the best time to talk to him. For example, if he doesn't want to be bothered when he first comes in from work, and needs to wait 30 minutes, just respect that and gently ask what you are needing from him. Learning the best time to talk to your husband will be something you must watch and learn about him.

5. Your husband is not there for your entertainment. When you got married, there is nowhere in the Bible that says when your husband comes home he is

supposed to entertain you and make you happy. You should be happy, because of your walk with God and looking for ways to make him happy when he comes home.

6. A man wants a kind, understanding, sweet woman, because the looks and beauty gets tired real fast.

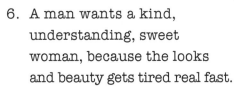

> 66 *You should be happy, because of your walk with God and looking for ways to make him happy when he comes home.* 99

These next pearls of wisdom are from a woman who was married for forty-four years. I remember the day I told Pastor Nancy I had feelings for a gentleman at my church. I was sitting in the church seats nervous, because I had these feelings bottled up for two years at that point. She smiled and looked at me and said I was in a season of preparation. Here were some of the things she shared with me:

1. When considering a man to be your husband ask yourself these two questions: Do I respect this man? Do I see myself serving him the rest of my life?
2. There is no perfect marriage.
3. My job is to help my husband, he may not be as scripturally strong, but naturally I could fill those weak points in him.
4. I said I wanted to be married; she said work on my relationship with God.
5. Don't try to explain yourself to an angry man (Proverbs 26:21-28). Wait until he can hear and do not take the offense.
6. I asked Pastor Nancy how to posture myself with male authorities. She said, "Always always come to him by

asking things in the form of a question." She told me to read the book of Esther. Every time she went to the king, she always asked in the form of a question in order to enter.

7. She told me to ask God what to do to prepare.

These next pearls of wisdom are from my friend, Amanda. She has been married for over 10 years. Here were her suggestions:

1. Know who I am in Christ.
2. Don't take things personal. Make sure to be flexible.
3. Care about the details of my outside beauty. Nails manicured, hair clean and trimmed, and feet polished. She said her husband mentioned that he liked it when her feet were polished and looked nice. Well she said that she did not keep up with them very well and one day she did her nails and he acknowledged how nice her feet looked. She realized that even though she did not keep up with her feet, he noticed when she did. So guess what, now she makes sure to do her feet all the time!

4. A husband will not continue to ask you to do something for him. He will address it maybe one more time then he will become silent. So make sure to complete the task that he requested and do it quickly.

> **❝Don't try to explain yourself to an angry man. Wait until he can hear. And do not take the offense.❞**

5. Make sure you know how to manage your time

better. Cooking, cleaning, and managing the household. Remember, it's not all your time anymore; you are there for the service of your husband.

6. Don't be moved by the actions of your husband; make sure to trust God concerning him.

Here are some recent pearls of wisdom from my two awesome sisters, Tina and Michelle. These ladies have been married a combination of nineteen years. Here's what they had to share:

1. Open communication is very important in a marriage. It keeps you both from holding in things that need to be discussed and keeps everything out in the open to prevent resentment and strife later on.

2. Do things that each other likes to do.

3. Listen when your husband comes in and wants to talk. Give him your undivided attention.

> "Don't be moved by the actions of your husband; make sure to trust God concerning him."

4. Don't get upset over little things.

5. In marriage, we should be like the daughters of Sarah and submit and respect our husbands according to 1 Peter 3:6, position yourself that he is your husband and authority.

Freedom Challenge

- What are some of the things that stood out to you?
- What could you apply to your life today?
- Who do you look up to for advice?
- Ask God what steps you can be doing in your life to get prepared for marriage.

Freedom Prayer

The Word says the promises of God are yes and amen. I choose to walk in the fullness of God, so at this moment, thank you for breaking all generational curses, past hurts, unforgiveness, and comparing myself to others. I thank you for creating me uniquely and delicately in my mother's womb just the way you wanted me to be. I love myself and I love you. You are a good God that wants the best for me. I will not feel guilty or ashamed anymore. No more condemnation or fear of others. I just choose to be myself and love you and others. May I be pleasing in your sight until I see you one day in Jesus' name. Amen.

Moving Forward

Whew...we made it to the end! I hope you have enjoyed driving along my journey with me. It is my desire that you learned from my mistakes, hurts, pain, low self-esteem issues, and consequences. I pray you saw how God helped to bring me out. I still have a lot of work to do, but I'm not where I used to be. I wanted to leave you with my final journey entry and a prayer over your life. This may be the end of this chapter in my life, but who knows you may see me again when I write another book about when my future husband finally gets here. Well, that's a whole other story!

7.17.2015

I find it fitting to finish my final journal entry in the secret place with the Lord. It was in fact where this book idea was birthed back in 2008.

Oh, how the journey took me in so many unexpected paths. Wide turns, the ups and downs, the bumpy roads to get me to a straight path to freedom. I finally see the light, because I made it to the end of the tunnel, forever changed by God's goodness and mercy over my life. I never thought at the beginning of this book I would make it to where I am today, but I say thank you Jesus! It was only God who was able to set me free. It was His Word that healed me. It was His hope that caused me to go another step believing I could be all He called me to be. It was His strength that held me when I wanted to give up. It was His love that healed the wounds in my soul. So I thank you God for all you have for me. I pray you ladies will be free and able to just simply be the wonderful self that God created you to be.

Freedom Prayer

Father, I am made whole and complete in my mind, body and soul. I am forever changed from the inside out and will know your goodness, your forgiveness and your love for me right now in Jesus name! I thank you God that I am free from every form of torment from past decisions and mistakes and have hope for my future. I bind you Satan and every lie, and every ounce of mental, physical, and emotional abuse you put in my life over the years. I command you to leave now and to never return in Jesus' name! I pray God that you give me the desires of my heart in due season. I am courageous and bold as a lion to say no when someone crosses any of my boundaries and that I stand up for myself. I declare that I prosper in every area of my life. And lastly, I pray I would know my purpose and that you formed me before time began for such a time as this in Jesus' mighty name. Amen!

Notes

Chapter 1

1. Dr. C. Leaf. 21 Day Brain Detox Plan retrieved from: http://www.21daybraindetox.com

Chapter 2

2. Business Insider 2013 – Bullying in America retrieved from: http://www.businessinsider.com/staggering-facts-about-bullying-in-america-2013-10

3. Bullying Statistics – Bullying and Suicide retrieved from: http://www.bullyingstatistics.org/content/bullying-and-suicide.html

4. Bullying Movements – Stand up to Bullying retrieved from: http://www.dosomething.org

Chapter 5

5. Daily Mail Article – Young Women Admit Regrets of Losing Virginity retrieved from: http://www.dailymail.co.uk/femail/article-2172305/As-young-women-admit-regrets-way-lost-virginity--Having-sex-young-ruined-love-lives.html

Chapter 8

6. Women's Health – Teens & Masturbation
   retrieved from: https://consumer.healthday.com/
   women-s-health-information-34/abortion-news-2/
   study-tracks-masturbation-trends-among-u-s-
   teens-655445.html

7. Wilson, P.B. (1995, p. 77). Knight in Shining
   Armor. Oregon: Harvest House Publishers.

Recommended Readings

The following list of books helped me along my journey of healing from my past and preparation toward marriage. I hope you find them just as helpful as they were to me.

The Great Exchange - Dr. Robb Thompson

The Approval Fix - Joyce Meyer

Ready, Set, Go - Dr. Robb Thompson

Knight in Shining Armor - P. Bunny Wilson

Bait of Satan - John Bevere

Wife's Role - Dr. Robb Thompson

Boundaries in Dating - Dr. Henry Cloud & Dr. John Townsend

And of course - the Bible!

65150949R00053

Made in the USA
Lexington, KY
04 July 2017